My adversary came onto the windowsill of another dream, as a bluebird

poems by

Michele Rozga

Finishing Line Press
Georgetown, Kentucky

My adversary came onto
the windowsill of
another dream,
as a bluebird

ACKNOWLEDGMENTS

"Yusef Lateef said: in India, you hear poems and prayers throughout the
    night," *The Comstock Review.*
"Time Bank," "Silence Cabinets," *The Comstock Review.*
"Last Night I Dreamed I'd Found Joey Ramone's i-Pod," *Rhino.*
"The Lifespan of a Sparrow," *Southeast Review.*

Deep gratitude for my theater, modern dance, and writing friends

Publisher: Leah Maines
Editor: Christen Kincaid
Cover Art: Michele Rozga
Author Photo: Jennifer Vetter, Exposed Moxie Photography
Cover Design: Mr. Donald Spencer, Communications and Marketing,
Norfolk State University

Order online: www.finishinglinepress.com
          also available on amazon.com

Author inquiries and mail orders:
Finishing Line Press
P. O. Box 1626
Georgetown, Kentucky 40324
U. S. A.

Table of Contents

*For the mothers and fathers who emerged
along the way, and for my family*

Little Ahab

This move, I lost the cover from my paperback of *Moby Dick,*
found the *Pan's Labyrinth* DVD I have been owing back to Netflix
since this past spring, broke two plates—one for food and one
for underneath a plant I have kept for eighteen years—my roots,

the things I truck around, include empty boxes
inside of the moving boxes. My new street's name is *Landfall,*
just at the edge of the salt marsh and an ocean-bound waterway
called Turner's Creek. The sky will be pink

then blue: tributaries mime its colors while white birds
flicker like feather brushes dipped in scarlet light.
The other books look small, on the shelves, they look damp
with a long journey, wordless now in front of our window

overlooking any next hurricane rising, target for the harpoons.
How to realize that you will never be satisfied with anyone
 who won't hurtle through space after the unknown creatures.
My hands curl around my life as if it might be an obsolete weapon,

one that's lost its nerve to kill. The raft dissolves,
sifting smoke just risen from the water and the reeds,
and your shoulder rests on my hip, your arms encircle my thighs,
storm now behaving like the maze at the center

of an order we are too small to see.

I.

Arrivals

Today, closed my eyes
for one minute, perhaps another,
in order to repeat the names of the people
I love, even
though estranged from some.
I love you, I love you, picturing those
faces, flushed and waiting
along the train station platform
that passes for my mind—my loves
congregating in me, a bodiless crowd.
Crowd says, don't write
about dreams,
their eyes wet with
effort, then they close them
to remember, their lids fluttering
inside my chest where a heart also sometimes
lives. And the rain comes. The crowd's hair
glistens as it did at birth.
Their cheeks are pink with pulse,
the rose sheds its perfume,
an engine of time breaks through.

Yusef Lateef said:
in India, you hear poems and prayers throughout the night

Bats chase insects against
ink blue fistfuls of thick sky.
The world tonight is an eye
lashed in sundown, a canyon
of sleep, a giant gone down
on her knees. Is this jazz,
this improv, the spring green
picked up and dropped into
a riff of no-color, now not reflected
in the prism? The crystal, stowed
away, knocks lightly in wind
that comes up, up, as of flight.

Sandhills break up between blades
in the spring. The house rides
the lawn like a wooden boat
the sea. A walk is a new thing,
the trees stride at the sides
of roads, their deities left behind.
The hippie in the India documentary
said *these people mistake nature*
for religion, so these bridging people
earn a hippie's distain. It's tempting
to cry when the nightfall keeps
falling, when the branches go still.

It's here. Don't look for angels.
When you look up, the clammy basin
of the early March night holds hard
plums of darkening stars, orange
feathers from passing galaxies,
talons separated from the hawks
that need them. So, the hunt takes
a rest, the settling-in is quieter
than the end of itself, so rightly
strange, the little girls next door have
lain down on the trampoline, its stretching
disk held still by their lightness.

Waiting, I become you in your absence

The small book,
        just finished, white cover, skulks

in plain sight on this café table
        outside the café.

Its cover is caught up
        by the light wind, its cover is

as thick as about five, no—ten,
        pieces of paper, but it bends

underneath the salvos
        of air currents.

The white cover shines
        as it reflects the sun,

the white cover shuffles out pieces of light,
        throwing them at the wind

as if it is throwing Mardi Gras doubloons.
        The prism of the white cover

blinds the black Labrador retriever Callie
        as she passes by.

The white cover, the air, the light
        make a circuit. My arm connects,

levers down and in, and there,
        a Post-it note in my pocket

scribbled with nouns:
        eucalyptus, lemon, sandalwood.

Now on a tree-vigil,
        my memory's sucked down

an alley of branches
        to where a foal stands

still, brand new in skill.
        A man takes notes

on a clipboard while the foal
        crimps all four legs, that accordion

of muscles it has one moment before,
        only just, learned to play.

The sound of what has been
        recorded is the squeal

of an old box fan which
        is the noisy cousin of celluloid

film running flat laps through
        its projector. Words

without these things
        hover, a force, over what might be.

The veterinarian wrote these instructions:
        stick the needle into a pinch

of the cat's neck skin, inject
        the fluids there to combat

dehydration. And even a cat
        might forget how to drink,

forget the feeling of thirst,
  give up the slaking for the dream.

And still, you're late.
  The bodies of the world are pushing

you farther away. I see you are
  trying to get here, to our café.

Our brains then just continuously equating

In the childhood of my language
the trees seemed to walk along
at the side of the road where I
walked. My mouth could barely
move because the blood in my
tongue so often just sang its song
without my help. The gods were
many and they weren't a big deal:
a firefly here and there, a snakeskin,
the smallness of a dollhouse
on the blue carpet at a dark-haired
friend's, a teacher who taught us
by just giving us the list of things
to know and do before Christmas. Tissue
paper flowers growing up in the halls
at school—a puffy forest we made, a place
to pursue each other. Then one more
ingredient: that seeing we did, of a friend's
house at night, from a distance, the safety
of a house lit up in all the widows,
teasing us to return through the splinter
of the cold air that was transformed,
by our inhales, into warm stinging bits of pop
inside our lungs, like sparklers,
our brains then just continuously
equating all of the words for joy with
all those curiously separate words for breathing.

Home

In late 2012, it was widely reported that a demolition crew in France had accidentally taken a 17th century chateau down to its foundation.

Brick by brick, the Chateau de Bellevue
came down. The Russian owner, by
radio accounting, was surprised when
he heard of the event from afar.

The workers saved the little shed
instead, the only structure on the property
actually given a death warrant.
Workers then could likely be heard

wondering about this turn of luck
in the open pits of the neighborhood
bars of Bordeaux. What were those
workers drinking while telling? Maybe

the wine of the region. Probably
they were laughing after having
a few too many, for their own
sakes, not for secret pleasure

at the mistake impossible
to hide, but for the pleasant
stony rumble they'd allow
to tumble around in their chests,

knowing that feeling— the
one that's so rare— when
the worst has happened,
and there's nothing that

can reverse it, the cleansing
of the eye, the stumbling
into the town streets,
the tears that can simply

fall as they're not going to be
seen. Also, the regret about
the holes in their socks where
the chateau's gravel got in.

The gravel could've once been
gold leaf, they might've thought,
or, the ashes and the burial urn that
held them, all democratic

particles now in the true marriage
of equals. The bodies of the named
stars—containers for fate and luck—
hovered un-housed over the workers

as they sobered up, got home. Then,
they slept and promised to remember
their dreams, which were of caves,
and paints made of blood and ground

roots, used to reconstruct raucous successful
hunts, the run across the green universe,
the awestruck place of the everyday
naked, the swerving but generous beast.

Heist

Because of greed, I imagine all the art thieves
tonight, not out yet, just waiting,

planning their ways through plate glass,
but right now standing in their kitchens,

refrigerators ajar (glimpsed through
gingham curtains, fat honey slices

of light and cold air) as the art thieves,
Edward-Hopper-like, probably

alone, decide on pickles for the relish
tray, chicken, green beans, sweet

potatoes. Van Gogh would not
have painted these art thieves,

as they are neither poor nor lonely
enough, here in the time before

they feast, slippered, at home, but
longing after hordes of Matisse.

These are the art thieves who would
sleep in the museums, if camping

were allowed, who would paw
through the painted drawers,

who would say: *my larceny
is my art, I'm only stealing back*

my belonging. Layers of paint
and solitude, the cries of millions

of pigments drown out
the better judgment

of the art thieves, who are not
civic-minded. After they eat

in the evenings, after going over
their plans, they do not go out

to cut the grass. Paintings, there are
always newly vanished ones: how

do the gorging art thieves decide
to try again to quiet this wanting,

when they so often seem to choose
the homely visions: villages after a war,

their fires banked down
under the filching plain brown

wrapper, suffering, sweat.
The right brush at the wrong moment

and an eye stays awake from a dead time.
Art thieves want a copy of everything,

the latest frail rendering of this life. Which
is all there is. So they take it, then they run.

Waking up

When it first happens,
the light is dim.
The purple sheets crimp
like shadows around you.
You are banished, by them,
to the Underworld, and it is hard
to get them to let go.
Because at least in the Underworld,
you might be a creature who
is walking through a myth.
Then, the dim light brightens,
you get out of bed,
stand still upon the earth,
then take steps into the world
of men, where hatred has been
hiding as you slept, as you tried
to get back to the home promised
in dreams, the home built of there.

Structures of the tongue

Take my hands, hold them so they remember
their use.

Take an ear, then another, play their bones,
give them song.

Take my spine, let it loose among some snakes,
this patience.

Take my knee, smooth it outside the river
of my body.

Take my wrist, shackle of the waking life,
jettison that.

Take my waist, take its measure, let the sand
fall through its chamber.

Take my scapula, place it in the reef I keep
to hope to lure you.

Take my thighs, those two ships, send them
to the deeps.

Take my mouth, take all the words it
used to contain,

take the place for bitter off my tongue:
show it to its new life.

II.

"Abandon normal instruments"

—Brian Eno, Oblique Strategies

Take a lover so you can put on clothes.
Sing your way out of communion with the adoring audience.
The holy wafer can also take you down.
Cut the bottoms off of whatever is being held up by your suspenders.
Arrange the flowers in the pencil cup,
then smear the pollen onto the dead white page.
Organize your thoughts.
Make something that feels so right, it undoes you,
then do that again until you drift away
as a blue neon electricity gathered up in the shape of you.
Put the pineapple right-side-up on that cake.
Your birthday should always be uncelebrated.
You are still in utero.
Your mother is a tiny girl.
Your father wears a sailor suit.
The ones you love, therefore, cannot die.
Now ignore even your brother, so he may also live forever.

"Shut the door and listen from outside"

—Brian Eno, Oblique Strategies

Do you remember ever seeing a closed door
and not wondering what hid on the other side?
A closed door tightens the senses, makes ears
and eyes into overachievers. The tongue, or
what it can taste, might be the only part of you
indifferent to a closed door, though cooking
from other apartments is also indifferent to doors.
          The psychology of a closed door depends
on your birth order, your existential shame,
whether or not you ever had your own room,
whether or not you have ever had something
to save.

          Past you, there is also the door to consider.
Is it yellow, gray, or tan? Is it round, double wide,
an elegant rectangle? Does the closed door close
you down, or does it, while it closes, excite
the pictures in your mind? Beethoven's door
was deafness, but he remained a musician.
What is the hardest thing for you, the most
impossible? *Do that*, says a closed door. Halls
of doors are like bullies taunting or diamonds in the rough.
          I prefer that doors stay on their hinges, but
I also prefer them ajar. When
they close, the Hoarded tend to mount in hills
of broken toys, raincoats, sachets, & sheets of music
out of order with their symphonies. But still,
there are all the individual notes to be rehearsed,
then played, no matter the listener, no matter
the longing for an overall sense of a master composition.
Listen. The color of that
is wide.

"Destroy nothing, destroy the most important thing"

—Brian Eno, Oblique Strategies

There is an order of holy men in India
who walk the roads and avenues and country
lanes in bare feet, continuously whisking a broom
across where they are about to step, so that
they don't accidentally take out any insects.

When the deep freeze hits, I secretly rejoice
in knowing how hard life will get for fleas,
how fewer and fewer of them will lay eggs
on my cats, carpets and grass, widgets,
pillows, that pair of Adidas left in the garage.

When I make things, I always pause too long
in memory of all the times I held back from
making. Sometimes I'm in despair, but sometimes
I can't make things because I think too much
about the destruction I will cause. Sometimes

I wish I could be a holy man, bent on honoring
everything in my path. I would walk and walk,
whisk and whisk, dust flying up, assembling in air
into the shapes of friends, and extinct species,
the screams of the righteous, humming of happy

elephants taking in the sun. Then, I want to
escape these thoughts, stride out and confidently
place my booted foot onto the soil, leave prints
deep enough to survive a heavy rain, deep enough
for any CSI to track, to say look! She was here!

There is an economy of gifts that lives outside
of what we buy and sell. In this type of system,
says my book, property and ownership kill
the very things they are meant to preserve.
Just picture dusty crowns in cases in the museums.

The gift economy says that the crown dies
the moment it is kept instead of being passed along
to the next worthy head. It is not making
something that destroys, but keeping what you've
made. Empty rooms reek of our treasures.

"*Remove specifics or convert to ambiguities*"

—Brian Eno, Oblique Strategies

The things I most remember from my childhood
are those things forgotten by my remaining people.

I asked my father about the painting of green
& blue brushstrokes, but he'd forgotten painting it.

I asked my mother what happened to the golf skirts
my grandmother wore in the 70s, the ones with red

rickrack trimmed edges and vigorous ladies
rendered in tiny, adorable appliqués. My mother

said, oh, we must have sold them with the house.
I asked my former self in the photograph, that girl

curled into a ball next to the sliding glass patio
door, color-blocked sneakers untied and the laces

trailing: what do you remember of your own
experience? She answered, not much I can confirm.

My youngest brother might still be a baby, crawling
across the kitchen floor of our house in Thibodeaux,

faded blue short overalls not covering the cast
on his calf from when the dog stepped on his soft

bones. My brother doesn't remember that wound,
preferring now so often to repeat the sentence I

don't need to know the specifics as a replacement
for how often the world has been indifferent

to his pain. And still, now in his unemployment, he
seeks a job and wishes to be useful, whatever might be.

III.

To be from somewhere, to say things about that place

In one town, there were more pawn shops per capita
than in any other place in the United States.
In another, I was small, rode my bike downtown
every day to stare through the college gate of Wellesley.

In one town, we were all novelties, some of the only
Americans, watched, not befriended, invited & avoided.
In another, there were ballet lessons after the long hot
dirty train ride, and the return at night, over the river.

In one town it was easy to sneak into jazz clubs under-aged,
and become part of the saxophone's swell and scream.
In another, the silence pooled in laps of moneyed houses,
and the people I knew were mostly prep cooks and maids.

In one town, we joined forces to steal liquor from a hotel
bar that bought in bulk and wouldn't miss it.
In another, we were invited after hours to a French
restaurant, and we drank their wine so gratefully.

Dreams run in real time

So, like any other's dream, it starts with a takedown.
The man who attacked me with a gun in the '90s strides

my way again, and I sidle under his swinging arm, grab his left
elbow like I'd grab the bar, palms up, on an approaching trapeze.

Then, I'm pulling him down, as if he were a lever on a giant
voting machine, with all my body weight. He forward rolls

over and behind me, banana, banana, banana, three windows
on the slot fill, so I'm the winner and the loser slink-walks away.

Once, my adversary came onto the windowsill of another
dream, as a bluebird. Therefore, I was to take the blue pill

and then fly to him, but I waited too long and the pill was only
sugar, did not give me the power to get on with it and forgive.

Postcard to a stranger # 1

What can be made of vinyl
is little grooves, spaces for sound
that turn round and round,
ready then to accept the diamond
point, dropped into the spot where
the voice goes when it hides.
There is a stack of records in many
places, secreted, recorded. In some,
Billie Holiday says, over and over,
as she did in the library in Colorado,
by way of the live recording done of her
at the Plaza, New York City:
don't explain, don't explain.
There.
Is where the music is.

Last night I dreamed I'd found Joey Ramone's iPod

A pink one, it was, the iPod:
I scrolled through the battalions of songs
as if I knew what to do, and found
Neil Young at the top of the list, a song
all by himself, and later on down
there was a band called *The Now*. Then,
in the dream, I had to run across the street
in bare feet to get a sweater—the now is cold,
Joey—but, I wake up and it still contains
Neil Young, Patti Smith, Bad Brains, inside
a flat pink pill box, like good medicine
bound in a saccharine safety-coat. Evidently,
my dreamtime scrawls a clef at the edge
of a landfill, but who am I to question
any strange bedfellows it unflinchingly swallows
while I nod off, allowing them to join together
under wretched covers, within its piles
of fish heads and Etch-a-Sketches,
instant mashed potatoes and un-raveling cassette tapes
dangling over-played pieces of *Boléro*?
After I go to sleep, a new body arrives
at the dump: shivering, alone at first, half-music/
half-banana-peel, it has to dive in, cover itself
with plastic bags, then continue to hold
its ground. Junk has a lost mother
too, who wonders about what has become,
but who tells about her kid, the most ugly, the beautiful
one, the naked one most far away from home.

His body's song

I have a friend who told me, last year,
that after the war, he'd read all of Proust's
Remembrance of Things Past.
All sixteen volumes. And so he never
needs to remember anything but music, ever again.

This friend had a Chicago friend, George,
and my great uncle was also called George:
my George was a bus driver
in Milwaukee. He had a union,
and, in the guest room, a self-playing piano,

but this piano still had a tuner, little George,
and little George was a long-haired
Black Sabbath who would never marry,
because he was too in love with his job,
which was, as I said before, that of music-tender.

This music he cared for came on pre-punched rolls,
and the waltzes and polkas were keyed up, showed
off at family parties, when George, little George,
and another uncle, Jack, hosted pit barbeques
and then said, *come inside—time for the show.*

And Jack, he kept a funeral home, and my
cousins all lived inside the rooms
above the laying-out parlor, but they were great
jokers, they were, and they even ate turkey
dinners there, and they made hippie jewelry.

George and Jack, and my friend—they each once
explained to me how everything steals away
from the business of living. Jack had a vacation house
on a lake, with a catamaran he took out cruising—
he'd often motor us silently to the other side.

Last year I watched my friend scale an eight-foot wall:
ex-Army-Ranger up, and get one leg over—
then he jumped off, a momentary escape, his body's
song completed by his refusal to keep up the fight,
and he hurried away, veteran music, old scars,

like the little boy who crooned, when my dog nibbled him,
that dog just touched my finger with his teeth,
instead of making the accusation: *that dog bit me.*
This is the problem. Not truth, not beauty, but:
Is the body a synonym for memory,

or a refutation of all it has survived?

Love songs in war-time

Tomorrow, there will be enough time
                  for you to be yourself,

    and so tonight
you are your kisses and you belong to me.

Tomorrow is on your shoulders, but now,
          this wait, our burdened wait. You—

    wearing a belt of regret: my hands around your waist.

I have always wanted to travel where I
am not supposed to go.

        In bodies we fly.
I know. Tomorrow, I will remember your face.

Once, I gave away milk and butter in the streets.
           Tomorrow I might meet myself

    again. Until then, there is
        another night, another that does not end…

…I had a house in Cabbagetown
        with a narrow back garden and chain link fence

    protecting these: an old camellia bush and a fig tree.
My camellias were red,

        every year, glowing knots of petals tied by February sun.
        But in August, the figs

    always dried up on the tree,
        into tiny hard gourds— inside,

seeds shaking, sounds of a snake's rattle tail…
Love, tell me why you are here,

in my new house tonight. I can't see your face.

No real harvest on the side of this road:
but still the return, tomorrow, over again, to this work, these

falling mortars, these lost legions.
So many sheaves to carry in, so many armfuls of stone.

Drone

This firefly, on dizzy maneuvers, who thinks you are its lost
lover, then hovers, blinks its light-bulb directly over your head,
on the off-chance
       you
have salvaged enough to blink
       back.

The lifespan of a sparrow

I thought I'd find it short,
just as the bird is small,
or even shorter than its size.
But some live on to twenty-five.

No sparrows alive when I was born
are still around, but it is not often
I stumble on the body of a bird.
This winter is a white shell,

lit only from within:
on the inside,
chisel of the forming beak
will hammer lightly into the sculpture

of itself, and one more bird, as if from ice.
Un-rumpling, wet feet, feathers,
our own heated yellow breath—
those bee stings inside new lungs,

the held trail of spark.
And these little incubations—
at Bailey's Ice Cream Parlor,
we gave all our change

to buy mint chocolate chip
in silver pedestal dishes,
Maria was the first Maria
outside of church we knew,

the closet at home cracked
open with tortoise and black kittens:
we picked them up, cradling them
to the unbroken egg-walls of our cheeks.

Salt harvest

The comedian in my memory speaks:
How do salt companies make money?
You and I buy only one canister of salt,
say, every two years or so. And the cost

is fifty-eight cents. But jokes always work
in spite of my telling, so: someone is mining
salt today, climbing a mountain of it,
white up the calves, glittering leg

hairs picked out by the mineral
hardening in damp air – here are
the stores of salt in everyone's cabinets,
waiting to be dished, or pinched, or thrown

over the shoulder after a bad date,
each grain tiny enough to get breathed into a lung,
disappear in the tissues around the alveoli,
little sacs of breath inside the pillars of us.

Turn and look, as your body precedes you,
back at your love, for loving is loving
before it is storied, or parable.
Most of our muscle never gets spoken aloud.

Helicopters over Cabbagetown

It was a windy fire: the old cotton mill
burning so badly the bricks themselves,
in the heat mirage, seemed to run down
the sides of what they'd once been.

No one slept for at least two days
after the fire was out, after the roofer
was picked off the top of a crane,
after the embers had finished flying.

Almost half a mile away, they said,
a shotgun house got taken down to its
odd narrow footprint on its naked lot,
and next to my shotgun, a piece

of scorched earth—*oh, yeah,*
my neighbors said, *we caught it*
before it touched your foundation,
and my dog was outside, barking

in the yard, stuck inside the chain-link
through this, the cat was under
the bed, where the air smelled of flames.
A famous photographer walked

around with his antique camera
and his girlfriend, snapping the people
who came in to sightsee while carrying
glasses of Champagne, nodding

to the remnants of our visible shells.
The next month, I found a pearly
dead squirrel in the rain barrel,
a piece of gray jelly in the shape

of a squirrel. It had fallen in,
then scrabbled the sides, I'm sure, before
sinking inside what it'd likely thought
of as salvation from burning.

IV.

Running toward the burning building

And the desk shook—he was telling her
there was a fire in Cabbagetown. How
he knew she lived there nobody remembers.

At first, she thought of the heater in her
shotgun house—it was old South,
an open flame gas unit—she thought
it might've caused the fire, then
the silent pictures on the TV
in the reception area—a funnel
of smoke, tall as skyscrapers,
and who-knows-what
being concentrated, being poured out

of the sky, or being poured up out
of what exactly burned in her neighborhood,
which, come to find out later,
was the unrenovated section of old
Fulton Bag and Cotton Mill, next
to the brand new pool for the condo's residents,
the pool she skulked into at night, until
they changed the gate code she had intercepted
by listening in on two people
 in the Cabbagetown Bakery.

            Jumped in the car, drove as far as she could
along the road beside the elevated train.
            One mile from home, the roads were blocked,
skies clear blue, the better to showcase
            the smoke-cloud. She parked, discarded shoes, ran
along the road beside the elevated train.
            The dog and cat were in her house.
She ran, lost an earring, an emerald green
            enamel one she'd bought in a fit of nostalgia
for her mother… for how her mother
            looked when she got to Paris
her junior year, that photograph of her,

black and white of course, wearing tiny
delicate shoes, pulling a mysterious suitcase
through the Metro Station.

She combed the weeds for a few seconds,
gave up the earring, ran on, and people began to appear,

groups of people who seemed to be
spaced at regular intervals, like the light posts

along the road beside the elevated train.
Got to a roadblock—nobody in or out, the cop said.

She told him. *My cat. My dog.* He waved her through.
The house, there still, gray of paint and of ash, only

a small burned spot in the shape of a rectangle next to it.
Her dog, barking at the chain link. Inside, smell of fire,

the cat under the sofa. Her belongings,
shrunk to the size of the closing aperture

of her eye: seeing all, unable to save any of it,
even if it had to, even if that eye had the time.

As if there were a ragged gemstone left over
in the center of what's burned.

Stretched on her bed, two years before
the Cotton Mill fire, eyes closed,
thinking back over the Timothy Leary
exercise she'd done earlier
that day, a planned
hallucination, the stuff,
she was told,
he did with clients
in late career

when he couldn't use acid
in the counseling room
anymore. The substitute stuff,
the breathing-into-a-paper-bag
stuff, until the blood becomes
hyper-full of oxygen,
and you, the breather,
the micro-chemical you,
the you that is a sandman
composed of debris from stars: you
begin to see all
things as if they were inside you.

So, this is what she'd
done in her creative workshop, this
is the way
she breathed too much oxygen
(as a fire does when
it burns) then hallucinated a cloud
in the shape of a woman reaching down
through a smoky funnel toward her as she lay on her back
in the attic of the workshop leader.

Having slowly crept back along the road,
beside the elevated train, and having gotten onto
her bed, two years before the fire, she saw with
her eyes closed, as she lay on her back, that her heart
was rising up out of her body.

Two years before the fire, the heat that houses in her
was hovering over her body,
held in place (right above the space it left inside her chest)
by a blue and purple rope of flames she was afraid would disappear
if she opened her eyes, the fire tethering the heart to her,
consuming her by tethering the heart to everything
outside of her, alongside the road that she walks,
beside the elevated train.

Time bank

In the time bank, there is nothing.
The time bank is a tiny porcelain sidecar
attached to everything you own
and everything you don't,

every person you even for once thought
about, even for one nano-particle,
every person you never knew,
every person you thought you were,

every person who thought he was you.
You don't have to move the time bank
from one camp chair or camp director
to the next—it does that for you,

for free. If you're very fast, you
sometimes will catch a glimpse
of the time bank cordless-drilling itself
or extracting itself from a sycamore's trunk,

or entangling itself or un-jamming itself
from the rubbery blond hairs of a plastic
baby doll. The time bank is not whimsical.
It doggedly clings onto prison walls for those

falsely accused. It replicates endlessly,
hasn't finished its self-creations. There's too
much to do, too much to notice. The time bank
is matter of fact about this work, not given

to much lamentation— if the time bank
could talk, it would say, *I must grow*
more selves, make sure to get emptier
each time, make room, make way, keep

the tally, keep up the shine on my buff,
catch and free the spawning salmon,
trade myself for a crumpled convertible,
fix it, then give those wheels away,

unspool the overly tidy invisible thread,
follow the bohemian waxwings
in the winter, the whooping cranes
in the fall, give everyone I find

the tiny hammer that can break
me into pieces when I'm ready,
the tiny hammer that can break me
into pieces when I'm full.

Scorpion

I heard it hit porcelain
with the rustle of the un-
complaining:

the scorpion, somehow inside,
had fallen off the wall
into the bathtub.

I was seven years old, my
sneakers on, still untied—
the closed door glistened.

It righted itself: curled
its stinger out of the way
of its feet, then over

its own back, then
it seemed to scream, measured
an inch of white

with its belly, then
another, then stopped,
smitten or stung,

on the unplugged drain.
I pitied its rage but
kept my distance,

clipped my chin over
the rim of the claw-foot
to stare down at my company,

the sad, wild thing.
And that was decades
ago. There is no antidote.

Lines

Two Figures II
Jeff Al-Mashat
Pulp painting on handmade paper

Two pregnant bellies made
of ultramarine blue lines: filling jars.
Pink lines triangulate over the blue,
in the foreground, as if little trails of silky
salmon-y fingerprint dust have been blown
over the stacked blue pots of stomach
to catch onto their growth, or
these are blue grapes, or cold-pierced tongues.
Two bellies of the painter's mind
fighting for space:
        oh progeny,
        I will protect you,
says the painter.
        And I wish I could say I also chose
        the man with the black teeth,
        his body huddled into the jar of itself
        as he smoked, offering us
        hand-rolled Turkish cigarettes.
        I would like to say I knew then
        that he was one of my many fathers.
Lines are tempered by their creation: closed in
seamless containers—
each line, at first, was started in search
of its end. But now all the beginning scratches
on the paper live secret lives:
hidden by their own completion,
the lines live as brimming vessels
live, because of the surrounding open field.

So many things I have
destroyed by this living. It is obvious to me they
are countless, they wait
patiently to be recognized—

for example, they wait on the street. And they wait here,
in this pink and blue
abstract by my friend:
Marks, I believe he said, *that's what I do.*
I just make marks.

Glass maker

Once I think I tried to copy
the sun with a piece of glass

and some saffron threads.
I drew and laced each orange

strand across the disc of the bottom
of a broken bottle, then crushed

them on the thick, clear-toothed
edge that never ended.

Saffron is from the harvesting
of stigmas of a purple crocus,

glass from the heating
of sand, or silica, along

with, sometimes, a thing
called pearl-ash, calling

to mind a latent sea awaiting
reconstitution by its own

water. The glass melted,
I thought, under the heat

of my hands, the saffron
burned itself into those waves.

And this was all while I sat
on the sidewalk, foot-soles

covered in mud, my name
thankfully not being called.

Every rider on the waiting bus

On the ninety-nine bus
from North Avenue Station,
riders. Most seats quite full,
with several persons standing.

Still, all wait— the driver
has not boarded yet. Outside,
a policeman's car pulls up,
a blue arm lowers its hand,

places a dollar bill
into the rubber collection
boot held by a fireman.
The teen-aged girl passing by

tilts her Doritos bag and spills
preservative crumbs on concrete.
She collapses the bag, passes
it behind her back like a basketball,

dunks on us by sinking it lightly
into the trashcan on the sidewalk.
Senses—there are five each
for every rider on the waiting

bus. About fifty people, times
five, makes two hundred fifty
pulses in each moment, crowding
up during this small delay.

There is a famous artist who molds
such common human forms out
of poisoned mounds of polymers
and clay. He doesn't even mind

that the life-sized man he made
to push a shopping cart in the museum
may be the one who kills him
while he waits for the grist: another day.

Silence cabinets

The walls of them groom the silence they shelter:
they finger-comb what has disappeared,
removing motes from light shafts,
or lovers from the stories they had parts in.

The street magician catches and buckles
another body into its bell jar, tending it
to fulfill the promise of illusion. The saw
chews in, but the body has become white doves.

The devil falls into a cave, streaming
noiseless fires, his voice stuck in heaven,
his sulphured fingers signing the words
for *there's hell to pay, and you have no alibi.*

Giants can't hear you now—the lost Titans
clash deafly, creating imaginary thunder.
On the radio, someone whispers *Golgotha,*
and then seems to swallow his tongue.

There is now less and less here of what
has fostered our senses, but there is a tree
that Hindus call the wish-fulfilling tree,
with branches that must be like a decision to sing.

A woman on a white horse

Waiting has no object.
The doorbell rings,
some Jehovah's Witnesses
arrive, their pamphlet

very thin, carrying
the title *All Suffering
Soon to End!* The images
of heaven on the cover

are bright and wholesome.
Two people, a woman, a
man, laughing with their
mouths open. In front

of them— as they recline,
clothed, in an alpine
meadow in summer— is
a small stand of poppies

or red tulips. Harvest
baskets nested in the flowers
overflow with squash
and apples. The seasons

are all beautiful, all at once.
There's a large animal
standing in the grass
behind the couple.

The visual dictionary
has neither a picture of
a caribou, nor a picture
of a moose, but the creature

on the pamphlet is one
or the other. Far away, but
striding towards the fore—
grounded couple, is a woman

on a white horse, riding
Western style. There's no
hint of what the darkness is,
of what needs to be overcome,

of what it is that will end. And
the conditions I know are only that
the ladies at my door are sweet,
plus they've promised to return.

How animals are courageous

Their stripes are their stripes are their stripes.
It is we who think of this as camouflage.
They are relaxed right after their predators
pass, because there is no time, for them.
They drag their prey past the places they,
in their turn, lost their kin, again and again,
but no malice. They need not be convinced
of the major keys of *love* and *hate* and *fend.*
They do not look outside for kindness.
If they can, they hide away when they are dying,
but waste nothing: most don't bury bodies.
Buddhists who ask to be put on mountains
after dying, to be left up to the buzzards, copy this.

V.

Nightingale says don't write about me

Though the dull brain perplexes and retards: Already with thee! tender is
the night...
>   John Keats

Did you look it up in the dictionary? In my copy,
beauty is: *arid, a night-tender that never leaves,*
is in the things most unlike you—peanut shells, tire
treads—or, beneath hay bales, alongside copper wire,
low on bus fare. It is also in the empty tin can buried up
to its crushed middle in desert sand after its short
flight from the hand that held it, then flung
it longingly into the cactus of empty arms.

Electric eel—defense of darkness

You cast the pulsing that is your net,
woven and tied of desire or thought,
need to eat telegraphed to your prey.
Once your hunger bumps against a fish,
energy devotes itself anew toward
600 volts—you send out the stun. Perhaps
it doesn't feel a thing when you swallow
it down to the bay where you hold silver
of your electric organs, tandem organs,
one for low voltage, one for high, plus your
electrolytes hovering together in the black
corridors of your body as it slips, flutters.
You prefer to live in darkness—your energy
does not emit light, and cannot be created
or destroyed, as you are a part of the Law
of Conservation: all Earth's energy destined
to remain constant, fluxing only by its
continuous transformations, potential switching
into sound, kinetic into heat, chemical into
radiation. Thick-skinned, your body hews
to the same current guiding any human hands
reaching at night to douse torches, rest
the eye. And your body is a type of rejection
of that individual hand that first dipped
a small brush into a dab of paint, and tried
to counterfeit, slowly, some white spark,
like the coming of another day into another
room. Light, traveling along human fingertips,
can't help but move toward the opposite of itself,
but you have your ornery, and conductive, resistance.

Rattlesnake

A fanging peel of Colorado cliff,
falling spiral off the knife
of evolution. Sharp and sudden,
pit in the grass at the side
of the trail.

We all stopped to stare at you.
You raised your head.

Art & animals

The artist gave a talk inside the magnificent building—
in Santa Fe, just off the square—about the body.
She used slides, projected paintings, and sculptures, of living
animals that have been used in works of comi-tragedy.

In Santa Fe, just off the square, about the body
of the thorned mesquite tree, whip-poor-wills,
birds that have been used in works of comi-tragedy,
came out for the evening light, to glide and wheel.

Of the thorned mesquite tree and its whip-poor-wills
the artist spoke, as she pointed to their display that one small life
could come out for the evening light, to glide and wheel,
could then be rendered by an artist's palette: the heavy scythe.

Lives, the artist spoke, and showed slides of each small life
permanently resuscitated in art, but forever lost to itself:
rendered by an artist's palette, a heavy scythe—
a hawk painting, a shark in a Lucite box, lithography of a rabbit's insides.

Permanently resuscitated in art, forever lost to itself,
each animal life, said the artist, expresses human limitations.
Hawk painting, a shark in a Lucite box, lithography of a rabbit's insides,
these are the ways we hold these bodies near enough for redemption.

The artist said her interest sprang from finding a murderer in her family tree.
She used slides, projected paintings, and sculptures of living.
All animals. She hounded her history through the works of so many.
The artist gave a talk inside the magnificent building.

In my museum

In my museum live all the machines that no longer work.
In my museum the mice bite, unscathed, into electrical cords.
In my museum, some of the paintings choose to hide out in the basement.
In my museum, each statue is missing at least one toe.
In my museum, pigeons fly through the broken windows, beg for crumbs.
In my museum, photos allowed, flash encouraged, lit cigarettes OK.
In my museum, the most innocent objects are rated triple X.
In my museum, dog hair has accumulated along the baseboards.
In my museum are all my enemies, come back as friends.
In my museum, the walls pulse with irritation at being ignored for art,
begin to plot revenge.

What need for that throat?

Gadgets, when enticing, have elegance.
This morning I found a birdsong identifier
machine. The machine plays recordings
of birds to people, so that any of them

can find out the name of the bird just
heard. At some point, the songs owned
for play on the identifier will become
second nature: to the person, to the birds

that overhear themselves being played
back to themselves. Once the song is
memorized, what need for the machine
that produced it? What need for that throat,

that beak, air, and vibration, or the pink
membrane, sputtering connection between
brain and body? But birds have astonishing
anatomies. They make more sounds than

humans are capable of making. The bird can't
be separated from the content of or reason for
its song. Each repetition surely has some tiny
necessary difference from each song that came before?

Occasional poem for happy

When there is happy, even this apocalypse
drips honey. We threw fallen pinecones into the fire

so their resin would powder up to scent
our campfire smoke. The quiet pond waited, its surface

content as the face of a grandfather. Kids jumped
into the parked RV, and swiveled in its recliners,

yelling: *I want this!* Tiny universe: only a few chairs,
a sink, a beige fold-out couch and bed, a steering wheel.

Each step we took began to seep a sap, as if the glue
of the world itself was loosening into a younger self,

as if sweet was not a flavor, but that thing holding
it all together at the seams. As if sweet, in spite of all,

was always the music fullest right before it's begun
to play, or candied tension ribboning the surface

of the coffee and cream, rippling out to the edges
of the mug you hold as you think about squeaky doors

that will soon be slightly soothed by a little of that
honey filling each & every crevasse in the metal

of their hinges. Some honey has come to rest
on the lumpy grass faces of graves, inside

the cups of flowers that grow from the cacophony of bones,
bones already ground down into the pollen powder

of another world, then eventually collected by the bees
and spun into honey, tithing for accidental days.

The disappearing man's self-portrait

Darling, I see you
have painted your face today—
I touch your cheekbones
as I touch the canvas
where your brush
was, just an hour ago.

Your paint is still warm,
as warm as the skin
over your cheekbones—
how did those apricots
get inside you,
did they slide down
the sloped backs of suns?

Darling, I see you
have painted your eyes today—
I tickle your lashes
as I brush the canvas
where your hand
was, just an hour ago.

Your paint marks, an open peacock
feather train— you: looking
out over our small rooms—

Darling, I see your yellow
shoulders speaking today—
they are the solar eclipses
of the whole year,
reversed, replayed:
backstage, you are all sun,

the bite of apricot.
Your pockets, in your painting,
are sagging, as warm
as the inside of a flown nest.

Darling, have you turned
them inside out,
searching?

Notes

Section II uses quoted directions written by Brian Eno during his time in art school.

The book cited in "Destroy nothing, destroy the most important thing" is *The Gift*, by Lewis Hyde.

The electric eel poem is inspired by a 1954 instructional movie made by *Moody Institute of Science.*

The name of the artist mentioned in *Art & animals* is Eugenia Parry.

William Utermohlen, an artist who painted self-portraits after being diagnosed with Alzheimer's disease, is the inspiration for *The disappearing man's self-portrait.*

Lines was written in response to a painting by my friend Jeff Al-Mashat.

Yusef Lateef made his remarks about India, inspiring the poem at the beginning of Section II, on the radio show *American Routes.*

After working in live theater and comedy improv in Washington D.C., and studying and performing modern dance in D.C. and Atlanta, GA, **Michele Rozga** attended grad school at Georgia State University and now works as an Assistant Professor of English for Norfolk State University. More recent publications include: "Ode to Little Houses," in the February 2018 Little Bird Press anthology *Where I Want to Live; in 32 Poems*, a May 2017 review of Josephine Yu's poetry book from Elixir Press, *Prayer Book of the Anxious*; poems "London Calling," "Spanish Bombs," in *Clash by Night*, City Lit Books anthology, May 2015; and a book chapter in Women's Studies and Film in *Migration, Diaspora, Exile: Narratives of Affiliation and Escape*, Lexington Books, 2020. Michele likes to take care of animals and plants, and has been practicing yoga for a couple of decades. She also likes to take photographs—an early publication of hers, in *Lumina* (Vol IX, 2010) was of a photo, taken at the Georgia State Fair on a clear and cold night during a full moon.

www.ingramcontent.com/pod-product-compliance
Lightning Source LLC
Chambersburg PA
CBHW021156090426
42740CB00008B/1121